TREES & CICADIDAE

Please do tell, How to forget you?

RATNA SETYA

Trees & Cicadidae

Please do tell, How to forget you?

RATNA SETYA

As Customers come and go, love
comes and goes even if you don't
want it
There is pain, wounds, puzzles,
and there are challenges and
laughter
And what those happened that
engraved in words is said to be
worth art, consolation, and
madness

Content

For The First Time

I'm holding your hands
Staring into your deep eyes
Touching your cheeks
Stroking your nose
Grabbing your hair
Kissing your forehead
And smelling your neck

Your soft lips
Your sweet skins
Your euphony voices
And your warm heart

Yes I am ...
For the first time
I finally see you
I see the whole of you
The Universe blessing you to found me
in you

Sweet Elegy

Hold your hand tight
I will not let go.
Hug your body tightly from your back
I want to freeze the time.

Smelling your fragrant body
A beautiful gift from the Universe.
Dimples on your cheeks
It is my lust.
The strength of your patience
Is addiction into my soul.
The euphony of your voices
Shattering my elegy.

I can't stop wanting you
I can't take my mind off you
I can't stop craving of you

I'll keep you in my vein
Burn you inside of my blood
I will be dazzling in paradise
So close your eyes
But i am dancing on my own
Blazing on my way
I've no reason to stay
Nobody, nowhere and wrack
So don't hold me back

You let me sinking with my reverie
This piece of something in you
Soft and tender
I need some space to breath

And this is the time
Let get this agony out
All I want right now is
I'm giving up on you
Cause I'm somebody new

Do not let me fall off your
dignity
Yet I'm questioning reality
How it will become to be
I lost my sanity

I could hold you, but I won't
I could chasing you, but I don't
I'm your virtual, then i'm gone

I've been sacrificing my infinity
Please do not drive me crazy

The chirping birds over the
branches
Chickens crowing at each other
The light orange gradation of
the sky
Emerging to the light blue
The big leaves of the Teak trees
Tabebuya waved pleasantly

How happy these birds are
The fresh air from the trees
Thank you Universe
For this wonderful morning

Infinity

Every breath away, I'm hoping
it's reality
Let me know if you are a
fantasy
Hallucination, I'm living in my
insanity
But you are my expectancy

Let me know when I should stop,
because you are all over me
Take my skinny heart
I'm lost, I'm your commodity

Let me hear your voice
Then I'll be your infinity
When we sailing away
Would you fight with me ?

A Litttle Tiger

She just a kid, a ten years old kid
Who have a big smile rather than
a falling tears

I'm sorry,
They are throwing away your
hopes
They think it is cool to destroy
other people life
They don't want to see you
growing up as a tiger

Dear little girl,
They don't control your anger
You are belong to your self
You are the architect of your own
life
So please continue your big
dreams

Vein of My Melody

Take me to the shore
I can't resist, I want more

You are the vein of my melody
Trap me, give me fantasy

Play my brain
Set me up, you are serene of
my insane

Beat my senses
I'm losing my consciousness

Found me
I'm nowhere I'm nobody

Euphony

The bright lights of the city
The haze of the dancing mist
The glamorous of happiness
The soft voices of whisperer
The sweet mind of harmony
The melody of embody

Euphony,
Is this a delusional ?

Rhythm of Mystery

The symphony of amatory
The endless of courtesy
The humble of illusory
The fairy of morning glory
And yet, the rhythm of mystery

Suave,
Yes I am surrender

Stubborn Head

And you...
The clumsiest girl
The annoying bookworm
The stumbling footsteps
The swinging mood
The counting sheep
The stubborn head

And yet, I am falling for you

Banana Leaf

I am not the one who will bring a
spare of shoes for you
I am not a mighty dragon who will
always carry you
I am not a shady tree that will always
shelter you
I am not the one who will carry an
umbrella for you
I am not a doctor who will bring a
medicine for you
No I don't

But...
I will be here to clean your dirty feet
I will carry you on my back
I will hold your head against the
shining sun
I will grab a banana leaf for you
I will always bring a band aid for your
wound
Yes, I will do

My Morning Forest

Hear... hear...
The voice of your little toes
The whispering of your soft lips
The swishing of your shining hair
Can you hear me baby?

Sniff... sniff...
The smell of your golden skin
The depth of your brown eyes
The agility of your fingers
Can you feel it baby?

My morning forest,
I'll be right here waiting
Under the same stars
Under the big pine tree
To always hold your hands

The Brown Eyes

You...
The little tiny god creature
Wrestling off my absolute
surrender
Whos never stop dancing in my
mind
Who dare to face this madness
Clumsy & stubborn
Who is coming against my turmoil
Who rip off my loneliness soul

You are coming melting to my
bone
You bring the scents of universe
You are belong to gorgeous smell
of the morning forest

Afternoon wind swept over the
sun
Your steps getting closer to mine
I need to keep my heart beat to
calm
Then we are ready to define
Because we are waiting this
moment will come

Standing in the corner of my chair
Hoping everyone will give us some
air
You and I are ready to bear
Erasing all doubts that we think
unfair

The universe is hearing my mind
!

Wait For Me

The afternoon's raindrops
The cold wind pierces to the
bones
Scattered leaves
The splashing footsteps over the
water on the road edge
My steps are chasing your bicycle
Hey wait..
Don't go down that alley!
Catch me!
Foolish!

I'm running toward & enfold your
shoulder
Dear the owner of a shady eyes
Dear owner of sweet chin
Wait for me!

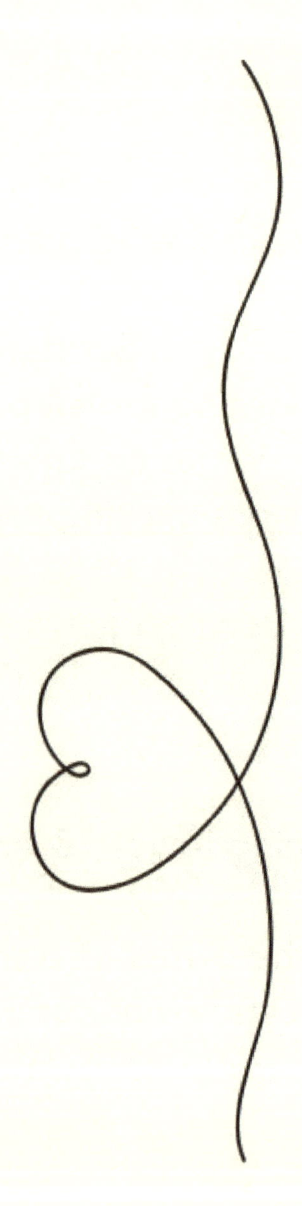

Rumbling feeling
The Raging of mind
A silent anger
And sometimes hating yourself of
being so far away from your loved
one

Throwing this doubt
Mean accepting heartfelt
Facing your own fury
Sometimes it get you melting to
the bone

Dear puffy eyes
It is okay to let this tears falling
Feel the misery
So can I start to hike up to the
mountain again?

The Wild and Shady Eyes

In the corner of a small cafe
Watching the sun goes down
The light blue sky
Turning into the ray color of purple
orange
Covering the wind & clouds
Bring me to a memory
When I always hold your hands
When I touch your closed eyes
It always coming back to this
I just want to lay down on you
And when you are opening your
eyes
I am looking the truth
The way you wink it
Your wild, yet your shady eyes
Should I say it will never been
enough?
Your pure of heart
Your pure of love

Trees & Cicadidae

The pink lotus
The fallen of white purple syzygium
Silver dragonfly flapping & grey koi
Boisterous of blue kingfisher &
cicadidae
Always reminds me of your evening
face

Please do tell
How to forget you

Missing you ...
Thinking to only about missing you
The one you miss is always busy
Busy at the outside, busy inside at
home
So, just immerse yourself into your
drawing
So that you don't remember the
missing

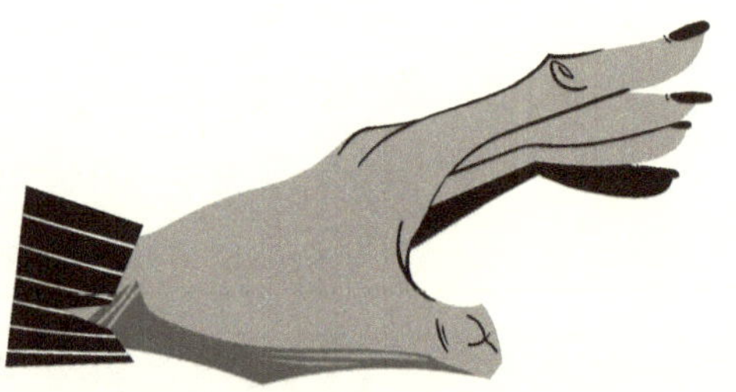

the writer is a woman who
was born in Jember, East
Java, Indonesia. She's an
architect. Architect of life
and love.

Ratna is addict to photography

Thank You
for reading

another poetry book
available soon